Stone Mountain

a walk in the park

photography by Larry Winslett

Bright Hawk Press, Dahlonega, Georgia

Bright Hawk Press
Dahlonega, Georgia 30533

Copyright © 2007 Larry and Julie Winslett
All rights reserved

Edited by Julie Winslett

No part of this book may be copied or reproduced in any form or by any electronic or mechanical means, including information storage and retrieval systems, without the written permission of the publisher, except by a reviewer, who may quote brief passages in a review.

This book is made possible by the Stone Mountain Memorial Association.

Printed in the United States

First printing, May 2007

ISBN 978-0-9755633-1-1

"People consider walking on water or in thin air a miracle. But I think the real miracle is not to walk either on water or in thin air, but to walk on earth. Every day we are engaged in a miracle we don't even recognize: a blue sky, white clouds, green leaves....."

~ *Thich Nhat Hanh*

View of Stone Mountain across Stone Mountain Lake

ABOUT THE PHOTOGRAPHS

Most of the photographs in this book were taken in the park's Natural District (see map opposite). Almost all are from areas easily accessible to the public and many will probably be recognized by park "regulars." Some photos, however, were taken in places that are off-limits to the public due to their extremely dangerous terrain, most notably the quarry areas and the steep south slopes. These photos make it possible for the reader to extend his ramble into places that are rarely seen. The images in this book represent nearly thirty years of "walks" in the park.

"To the attentive eye, each moment of the year has its own beauty...it beholds, every hour, a picture which has never been seen before, and which shall never be seen again."

~ Ralph Waldo Emerson

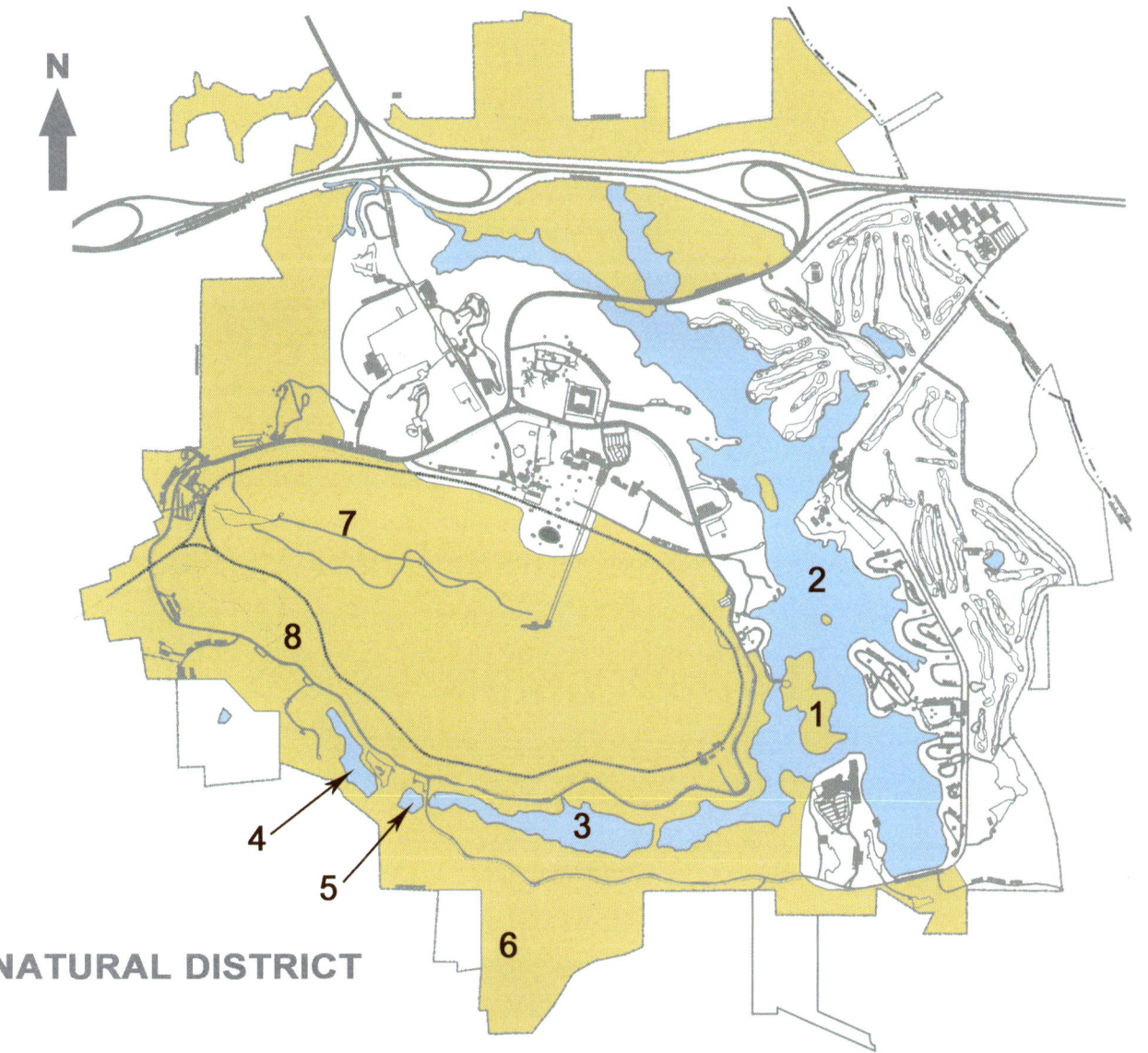

NATURAL DISTRICT

In 1995, the Georgia Legislature enacted measures that set aside the highlighted areas as Stone Mountain Park's "Natural District." These areas contain many wildlife habitats and are protected from future development. They include streams, lakes, rock outcrops, native forest, and fields. Most of the park's trail system is also within these areas, including the Walk-up Trail (7) and the historic Cherokee Trail around the mountain. Other important sites are Indian Island (1), Stone Mountain Lake (2), Venable Lake (3), Howell Lake (4), the Catfish Pond (5), the Bird Habitat (6), and the Nature Garden (8). As new properties are added to the park, they will be considered for inclusion in the Natural District.

FOREWORD

The Stone Mountain Memorial Association was created by the Georgia General Assembly in an act signed by the Governor on February 21, 1958. The purpose of the Association was to acquire and manage Stone Mountain Park as a memorial to the Confederacy and as a place of public recreation.

The "memorial" part of the Association's mission has been accomplished through the completion and maintenance of the world's largest bas relief carving depicting Jefferson Davis, Robert E. Lee and Stonewall Jackson. The Antebellum Plantation and the Memorial Hall museum also contribute to this mission.

The "public recreation" part of the Association's mission has been met through the development of attractions (e.g., Stone Mountain Lake, the aerial tramway, and riverboats), walking trails, festivals, and, more recently, an environmental and historical education program.

Throughout its existence, the Association has had to deal with tensions inherent in the purposes it serves. It must provide a fitting memorial to those who made great sacrifices and fought with valor for a cause they believed in while also condemning the evils of slavery and oppression that accompanied that cause. It must provide recreation/entertainment opportunities in a way that makes it financially self-supporting without impinging too much on the natural beauty of undeveloped woodlands and open spaces.

The Association stands to be judged every day on its success or failure in managing these tensions. As the Association approaches its fiftieth anniversary, this publication is an effort to "bookmark" the park – to record what it looks like in the first decade of the twenty-first century. Hopefully, it will provide an overview of the park to assist all of us in judging how we have managed so far and a baseline for future generations to evaluate how well they succeeded in taking care of one of Georgia's greatest natural resources.

The Association expresses its great appreciation to Larry and Julie Winslett, whose love of the park and whose dedication and hard work have made this publication possible.

G. Curtis Branscome, May 2007

Covered Bridge on the Cherokee Trail

INTRODUCTION

Walking through Stone Mountain Park's forests and by its lakes, one can easily forget that Atlanta is less than twenty miles to the west. Because of its urban location, Stone Mountain is sometimes overlooked as one of Georgia's, and the nation's, great natural wonders. As the planet's largest exposed solid granite outcrop, or monadnock, it has even been called one of the natural wonders of the world. Created in 1958, the Park has seen many changes over the last fifty years. But despite the changes that time and man have brought about, an abundance of natural beauty remains today and Stone Mountain's importance as a natural history site is undiminished. Surrounding the mountain are a plethora of rock outcrops, forests, streams, and lakes – natural features that can rarely be found all in one park, especially in an urban area. The park is home to hundreds of species of flowering plants and boasts one of the highest concentrations of biological and habitat diversity in the state. Many of the plant species here are extremely rare, including one of the world's rarest plants, the Black-Spored Quillwort, which can be found in the shallow pools on the mountain's summit. The park is also home to some of metro Atlanta's only remaining old-growth forests. It would be impossible to overstate the natural significance of Stone Mountain, and visitors who overlook the natural areas are missing a real treasure.

Stone Mountain Park is also a paradise of opportunity for photographers. Due to the mountain's elevation relative to its surroundings, incredible views can be seen from the top. Sunrises and sunsets can be especially spectacular. The park's hundreds of species of flowering plants, ferns, mosses, trees, and mushrooms and other fungi offer abundant opportunities for studying nature's wonders in all seasons. Wildlife is a bit more elusive, but deer, rabbit, fox, squirrels, raccoons, and many species of insects can be found here. The variety of bird life in the park is especially impressive. The weathered and constantly changing rock surfaces also offer an endless array of interesting patterns and geological features. The wildflower display in spring and fall is the true highlight for nature lovers. In good years, the explosion of Yellow Daisies provides one of nature's great sights, turning whole sections of the mountain into brilliant rivers of gold.

For me, working on this book was like walking back in time. After spending nearly thirty years photographing the park, I found it interesting to look back at the images from long ago and see how the park has changed. It was also a moving experience for me to reminisce with people I met on the trails as I revisited areas of the park looking for new images for this book. People come here for many reasons – solitude, recreation, spiritual healing, or simply to walk the dog or spend time with friends. When folks I met found out what I was doing, their stories of the park came gushing out. There were lots of "do you remember when" and "have you ever seen" moments. They told me of their adventures in the park, and their love for it. Their experiences reminded me of my own – quiet afternoons, walks along swift, rain-fed streams and through cool green forests, autumn colors, lush lakeshores, summer breezes, memorials carved in stone to lovers and the departed, hawks and vultures floating above, or simply sitting among fields of brilliant flowers. The experience of Stone Mountain Park affirms the truth of John Muir's words – "In every walk with nature, one receives far more than he seeks." It is my sincere hope that the images on the following pages capture a little of that wonder and spirit for you to enjoy as you "walk" through the park in this book.

Larry Winslett, May 2007

Sunset on Stone Mountain Lake

Stone Mountain reflected in Venable Lake

"Climb the mountains and get their good tidings. Nature's peace will flow into you as sunshine flows into trees. The winds will blow their own freshness into you... while cares will drop off like autumn leaves."

~ John Muir

Erosion patterns near the summit

"Our way is not soft grass, it's a mountain path with lots of of rocks. But it goes upward, forward, toward the sun."

~ Ruth Westheimer

Boulders and loose rock on the south slopes

Pines on the south slope

"An early morning walk is a blessing for the whole day."
~ Henry David Thoreau

Quarried areas on the south slope

The effects of erosion and weathering

Scenes from the north (this page) and south slopes

Yellow (Confederate) Daisies on the south slope

"The earth laughs in flowers."
~ Ralph Waldo Emerson

Yellow Daisies and Blazing Star on a north outcrop

Scenes at the bases of the south and north slopes

Exfoliating rock and foamy pools at the base of the north slope
(the foam consists of granite particles and loose soil picked up by
the rain as it washes down the steep slopes)

Along trails in the park

"The winding path approaches the secluded and peaceful place."

~ Huang Binhong

Early homesteads

*"And as I pass by these old abandoned places,
I wonder about the stories they could tell,
and wish I could see their faces,
and I wonder about their names."*
~ Unknown

Streams feeding Venable and Howell Lakes

"Like dreams, small creeks grow into mighty rivers."
~ Willa Cather

Cascade on Little Stone Mountain Creek

"Water is the driver of nature."
~ Leonardo Da Vinci

Rain-fed stream in the Nature Trails area
(note the two depressions in the rock that were used by Native
Americans as mortars for grinding food)

Streams in the Nature Garden

Stream connecting Stone Mountain Lake and Venable Lake
and view of the mainland from Indian Island

Stream north of Highway 78
and temporary rain-fed pond at one of the quarry sites

Rock arrangements near the quarry pond and stepping stones in the American Pen Women site

Names carved in stone

Early autumn on Venable Lake

Turtles, sumac, and wetlands

Summer and autumn on Venable Lake

Winter on Howell Lake

Autumn woods

Autumn and summer on the shores of Stone Mountain Lake

Looking skyward through pines and maples

Pileated Woodpecker and the Bird Habitat

"In summer when I passed the place,
I had to stop and lift my face;
A bird with an angelic gift
Was singing in it sweet and swift."
~ Robert Frost

Rock Aster, Wild Indigo, Horse-nettle, Yellow Daisy, Blue-curl, Autumn Bells, and Wild Columbine

"For myself I hold no preference among flowers, so long as they are wild, free, spontaneous."

~ Edward Abbey

Rabbit, Luna Moth, lizard, and squirrel
(many species of mammals, birds, reptiles, amphibians, fish, and insects live in the park)

Canada geese, Mallard duck, and Great Egret

Mosses, lichen, and rain-fed stream

Fungi and lichen, pollen, red diamorpha, and moss on a rock outcrop

Views of Stone Mountain above Stone Mountain Lake

"I come into the peace of wild things who do not tax their lives with forethought of grief... For a time I rest in the grace of the world, and am free."
~ Wendell Berry

Woods and the Catfish Pond in the fall

Sumac and autumn trees at the campground

"Autumn is a second spring where every leaf is a flower."
~ Albert Camus

Waning moments of autumn on Stone Mountain Lake

"Autumn, the year's last, loveliest smile."
~ William Cullen Bryant

Autumn reflections on Venable Lake

Virginia Creeper and autumn woods

Sunrise on Stone Mountain Lake
and sunset on Venable Lake

"My first thought is always of light"
~ Galen Rowell

Dawn on the mountain and at the golf course

Sunset at Stone Mountain

You have just taken a "walk" in Stone Mountain Park in the first decade of the twenty-first century. But people have been walking in what is now the park since at least 6000 BCE. From the prehistoric indigenous peoples who lived here to the Creek Indians and European settlers of the last few centuries, to the people of today, Stone Mountain has served humans as home and spiritual haven for thousands of years. The park is one of the most visited in the United States, and for good reason. In addition to a host of entertainment and shopping attractions, it also offers the world of nature, with its own host of attractions for those seeking peace, beauty, and spiritual refreshment. And that is what the "walk" in this book attempts to illustrate. Now that you have taken this "walk," we hope you will take a real walk in the natural areas of Stone Mountain Park and experience for yourselves the wonders that are offered here.